Ahlam Gouda

Introduction of research Methods in Nursing

Ahlam Gouda

Introduction of research Methods in Nursing

Noor Publishing

Imprint

Any brand names and product names mentioned in this book are subject to trademark, brand or patent protection and are trademarks or registered trademarks of their respective holders. The use of brand names, product names, common names, trade names, product descriptions etc. even without a particular marking in this work is in no way to be construed to mean that such names may be regarded as unrestricted in respect of trademark and brand protection legislation and could thus be used by anyone.

Cover image: www.ingimage.com

Publisher:
Noor Publishing
is a trademark of
International Book Market Service Ltd., member of OmniScriptum Publishing Group
17 Meldrum Street, Beau Bassin 71504, Mauritius

Printed at: see last page
ISBN: 978-620-0-06107-2

INTRODUCTION OF RESEARCH METHODS IN NURSING

Prepared by
Dr/ Ahlam Gouda

Research Methods in Nursing

Content outline:

I: Overview about research & research in nursing

-Definition of research methodology

- Definition of nursing research

-Importance of research in nursing

II: Research process

- Select a topic

- Review existing research and theories that are relevant

- Develop a hypothesis or research question/s

- **II: Research process**

-Research project

- **Research designs:**

- *Observational research designs*

a- Descriptive research design:

- Cross- sectional study design

- Qualitative research design

b-Analytical research design

- *Experimental research design:*

- Randomized control trails

- Quasi experimental design

Unit IV: Data collection

- Tools and methods of data collection

- Sampling

Unit V: Research Ethics

Introduction about nursing research

I: Overview about research & research in nursing

- **Def. of research methodology**
- **Def. of nursing research**
- **Importance of research in nursing**
- **Research project**

II: Research process

- **Select a topic**
- **Review existing research and theory that are relevant**
- **Develop a hypothesis or research question/s**

Definitions for research

Methodological investigation used to discover facts, to establish or to develop a plan of action based on facts discovered.

OR

Research is the collection of information (data) to obtain more knowledge or to answer a specific question about a certain topic.

Nursing Research

Research is systematic inquiry that uses disciplined methods to answer questions or solve problems. The ultimate goal of research is to develop, refine, and expand a body of knowledge.

Importance of research in nursing

- ❖ It validates nursing as a profession.
- ❖ It provides a scientific basis for nursing practice.
- ❖ It demonstrates accountability of the profession.
- ❖ To develop a scientifically based body of knowledge unique to nursing
- ❖ To answer questions
- ❖ To solve problems
- ❖ To improve the quality of care
- ❖ To advance nursing as a profession

Research Process

7 Basic steps of research process:

1. Select a topic
2. Review existing research and theory that are relevant
3. Develop a hypothesis or research question/s
4. Determine the appropriate methodology/research design
5. Collect relevant data

6. Analyze and interpret the results

7. Present the results in an appropriate form

Factors to consider in the choice of a research topic

1. Novel

In the event that the problem has been studied before Inject originality in it by coming up with another research design by: Using a different data-gathering tool **OR** a different scheme for analyzing the research data.

2. Interesting

3. Relevant

The results of the study on a given problem should be:

Practical value to the researcher and the significant others in the field.

Will the results add knowledge to information already available in the field?

4. Feasible – This means that a problem that the research problem can be completed without: undue amount of time, money or effort. The researcher has the necessary competence or expertise to conduct the study on the chosen problem.

<u>Examples:</u>

Is the topic too broad? (e.g. the effects of TV violence on children)

Can the problem really be investigated? (e.g. availability of information)

What costs and time are involved in the analysis?

5. Researchable – Data can be collected to answer the problem posed

by the researcher.

Can the data be analyzed? (Can the data be measured?)

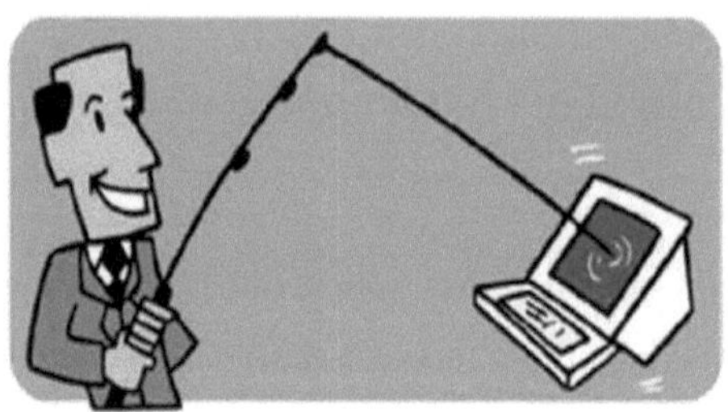

6. Ethical –   A problem is

said to be ethical when it does not involve physical or psychological

harm or damage to human beings or organizations.

2- Reviewing the Literature

What other researchers have done in relation to the topic to be studied?

<u>Purpose:</u>

1. Broaden the researcher's knowledge base in research area;

2. Ensuring originality in the conduct of one's research

3. Ensuring clarity and focus on one's study

4. Provide the researcher insights on the weaknesses and strengths of previous studies

5. Provide findings and conclusions of past studies, which researcher can use in relating to his own study.

6. Help the researcher in formulating the theoretical and conceptual framework for his research problem.

<table>
<tr><td>

Guidelines in doing the Review

</td><td>

</td></tr>
</table>

1-Search for existing literature in the library and on the web

Prepare a working bibliography. Record all vital details concerning the books or research you are including in your bibliography

2-Write in 3x5 index cards; group together references from

    a. books

    b. journals and periodicals

    c. unpublished material

3- Examine each material, and then decide which ones will actually be included in your review.

<u>Characteristics of the Review</u>

1. The text of the review should be brief and to the point.

❖ To ensure brevity and conciseness,

❖ Summarize or paraphrase important points

❖ Avoid direct quotations of the author's ideas or the results of the studies you are reviewing.

2. Have a plan on how to present the review. Prepare an outline before finally writing the review

Writing the Review

Approaches to presenting the review:

1. Chronological

Literature and studies are presented according to the year they were written. Sample outline:

- Introduction
- Recent literature & studies
- Least recent literature & studies
- Synthesis of the review

2. Thematic

Literature and studies with the same findings are grouped together. Sample outline:

- Introduction
- Literature & studies on Variable 1
- Literature & studies on Variable 2
- Synthesis of the review

3. Country of origin

Literature and studies are categorized based on the country/continent where they came from. Sample outline:

- Introduction

- Foreign literature & studies

- Local literature & studies

- Synthesis of the review

3. Develop a hypothesis or research question/s

A research questions is a statement of specific query the researcher wants to answer to address the research problem.

OR

It is a statement of problem that the researcher would like to research.

Characteristics of Good Research Questions:

1. The question is feasible
2. Significant
3. The question should be of your interest
4. The question should be researchable
5. Ethical
6. The question is clear

Research Question (examples)

- ✓ What is the relationship between the dependence level of renal transplant recipients and their rate of recovery?

✓ What are the coping strategies used by husbands and wives to deal with their infertility?

✓ How do nurses perform in infection control measures?

4. Research Hypotheses

- Researcher hypothesis is a prediction of the expected relationship between two or more variables.

- It can be seen as proposed solutions or answers to research question.

- Hypotheses should be based on sound, justifiable rationale.

- A good hypothesis should be consistent with an existing body of research findings.

A hypothesis expresses an expected relationship between independent variable and dependent variable.

Independent variable:

- The variable that is believed to cause or influence the dependent variable.

- In experimental research, it is the variable that is manipulated and controlled by the researcher (e.g. treatment).

Dependent variable:

- The outcome variable / the effect.

- The variable that is caused by the independent variable.

Examples of Research hypotheses

- o Excessive dietary salts intake (**Independent variable**) resulting in elevated blood pressure (**Dependent variable**)
- o Renal failure is a complication of untreated urinary tract infection

Characteristics of good hypothesis

1. Simple language
2. Concise
3. Provides definition of the variable
4. Operational terms:

Research Questions vs. Research Hypothesis

- *Question:* Does room temperature affect the optimal placement time of rectal temperature measurements in adult?
- *Hypothesis:* Cooler room temperature requires longer placement time for rectal temperature measurements in adult than warmer room temperature.

---

4. Determine the appropriate methodology/research design

A research design is the heart and soul of a research project. It outlines how the research project will be conducted and guides data collection analysis and report preparation. A good research although forms broad approach to the problem that has already been developed and research design specifies the nuts and bolts of implementing that approach.

Definition of research design

According to Naresh Malhotra:"The research design is a framework or blueprint for conducting the research project".

According to Chris Jordan: "The research design is a blueprint for conducting the study that maximize control over factor that could interfere with the validity findings".

Purpose of research design

- Provides the plan or blueprint
- Is the vehicle for systematically testing research question and hypotheses
- Provide the structure or maintaining the control of the study

Components of research design

Research design involves the following components as follows :

1. Design the exploratory, descriptive and causal phases of the research .
2. Define the information needed .
3. Specify the measurement and scaling procedures .
4. Construct and pretest a questionnaire or an appropriate form for data collection .
5. Specify the sampling process and sampling size .
6. Develop a plan of data analysis .

Characteristics of a good research design

The following are the characteristic features of good research design:

1. Appropriate for research question: The research design should be appropriate for the questions being asked.
2. Free from bias: A good research design will collect and store data which is not biased.

3. Precise refers to the appropriateness and accuracy of the statistical procedures used to analyze data.

Classification of research design

The research design is broadly classified under to headings as follows:

A. Quantitative research

Quantitative research refers to the systematic empirical investigation of quantitative properties and phenomena and their relationships.

The objective of quantitative research is to develop and employ models, theories and/or hypotheses pertaining to phenomena.

The process of measurement is central to quantitative research because it provides the fundamental connection between empirical observation and mathematical expression of quantitative relationships.

B. Qualitative research

Qualitative research design aims to gather an in-depth understanding of human behavior and the reasons that govern such behavior.

The qualitative method investigates the why and how of decision making not just what, where and when. Hence, smaller but focused samples are more often needed, rather than large samples.

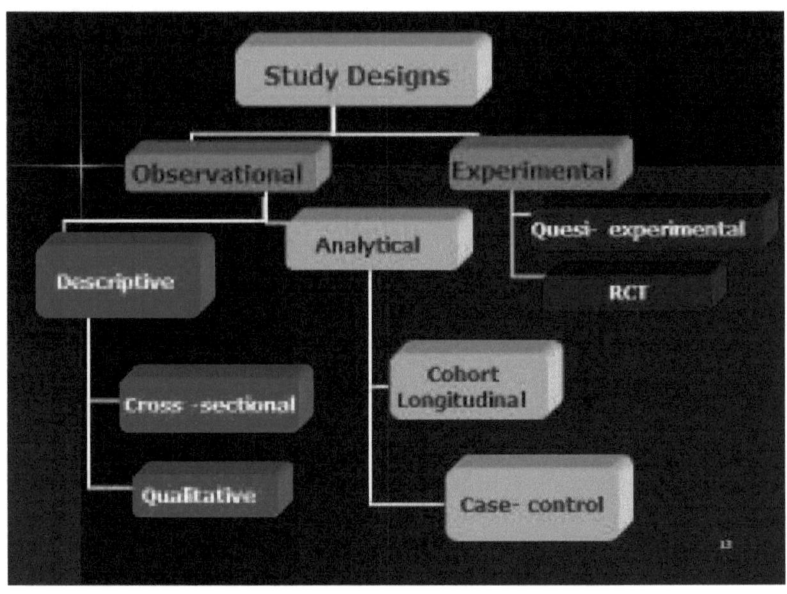

Differences table between qualitative and quantitative research

Items	Qualitative Approach	Quantitative Approach
Definition	Qualitative research design aims to gather an in-depth understanding of human behavior and the reasons that govern such behavior. Qualitative research is a method of inquiry that develops understanding on human and social sciences, to find the way	Quantitative research refers to the systematic empirical investigation of quantitative properties and phenomena and their relationships. Quantitative research is a research method that is used to generate numerical data and hard facts, by employing

	people think and feel.	statistical, logical and mathematical technique.
Nature	Holistic	Particularistic
Approach	Subjective	Objective
Research type	Exploratory	Conclusive
Reasoning	Inductive	Deductive
Sampling	Purposive	Random
Data	Verbal	Measurable
Inquiry	Process-oriented	Result-oriented
Hypothesis	Generated	Tested
Elements of analysis	Words, pictures and objects	Numerical data
Objective	To explore and discover ideas used in the ongoing processes.	To examine cause and effect relationship between variables.
Methods	Non-structured techniques like In-depth interviews, group discussions etc.	Structured techniques such as surveys, questionnaires and observations.
Result	Develops initial understanding	Recommends final course of action

Another frame of differences table between qualitative and quantitative research

Items	Quantitative Approach	Qualitative Approach
Scientific method	Deductive or "top-down" Test hypothesis and theory with data.	Inductive or "bottom-up" Generate new hypotheses and theory from data collected.
Most common research objectives	Description Explanation Prediction	Description Exploration Discovery
Focus	Narrow-angle lens Testing specific hypotheses	Wide and Deep-angle lenses Examine the breadth and depth of phenomenon to learn more about them.
Nature of study	Study behavior under artificial, controlled conditions.	Study behavior in its natural environment or context.
Form of data collected	Collect numeric data using structured and validated instruments (closed-ended survey items, rating scales, measurable behavioral responses)	Collect narrative data using semi- or unstructured instruments (open-ended survey items, interviews, observation, focus groups, documents)
Nature of data	Numeric variables.	Words, images, themes, and categories
Data analysis	Identify statistical relationships.	Holistically identify patterns, categories, and themes.

| **Results** | Generalizable findings. General understanding of respondent's viewpoint. Researcher framed results. | Particularistic findings. In-depth understanding of respondent's viewpoint. Respondent framed results. |
| **Form of final report** | Statistical report including correlations, comparisons of means, and statistically significant findings. | Narrative report including contextual description, categories, themes, and supporting respondent quotes. |

Quantitative study design classification

Several classifications of quantitative study types are possible, depending on what research strategies are used.

1. Intervention studies in which the researcher manipulates objects or situations and measures the outcome of his manipulations (e.g., by implementing intensive health education and measuring the improvement in immunization rates.); and

2. Non-intervention (Observational) studies in which the researcher just observes and analyses researchable objects or situations but does not intervene

Experimental designs (Intervention studies)

In intervention studies, the researcher manipulates a situation and measures the effects of this manipulation. Usually (but not always) two groups are compared, one group in which the intervention takes place (e.g. treatment with a certain drug) and another group that remains 'untouched' (e.g. treatment with a placebo).

Experimental design is a powerful design for testing hypothesis of causal (cause-and-effect) relationships among variables because they help eliminate potential threats to internal validity.

To infer causality requires that these three criteria be met:

- The causal (independent) and effect (dependent) variables must be associated with each other.
- The cause must precede the effect.

- The relationship must not be explainable by another variable.

Experimental designs classifications

Experimental designs may be classified as

1. True Experimental
2. Quasi-experimental
3. Pre-experimental

Frist: True experimental design (A randomized controlled trial)

A randomized controlled trial is an epidemiological experiment designed to study the effects of a particular intervention, usually a treatment for a specific disease.

In an experimental study, subjects are randomly allocated to at least two groups. One group is subject to an intervention, or experiment, while the other group(s) is not. The outcome of the intervention (effect of the intervention on the dependent variable/problem) is obtained by comparing the two groups.

Uses

- These are widely used in laboratory settings and in clinical settings.
- For ethical reasons, the opportunities for experiments involving human subjects are restricted.
- However, randomized control trials of new drugs are common.

Characteristics of true experimental design

A true experimental design consists of the following three characteristics:

1. Manipulation

It refers to conscious control of the independent variable by the researcher through treatment or intervention(s) (doing something) to observe its effect on dependent variable.

In other words, it is a conscious act by the researcher, he or she or varies the independent variable and observes the effect that manipulation has on the dependent variable of interest.

Example (1)

Suppose we hypothesize that gentle massage is effective as a pain relieve measure for elderly nursing home residents. Providing gentle massage to elderly in experimental group and withholding for others in control group is considered manipulation of independent variable, where the effect of this manipulation is observed on the pain level in both the groups.

Example (2)

In a study of the effects of preoperative teaching, the situation might be manipulated, so that one group of subjects received preoperative teaching and another did not.

2. **Control**

Control refers to the use of control group and controlling the effects of extraneous variables on the dependent variable in which the researcher is interested. The subject in the control and experimental group are similar in number and characteristics, but

the subjects in the control group receive no experimental treatment or any intervention at all.

The experimental group receives the planned treatment or intervention and a comparison is made with the control group to observe the effect of this treatment or intervention.

Control group has three types as the following:

Negative control: In this type of control group, the subject neither receives any placebo or other type of treatment or intervention.

Clear control: The subjects in this type of control group receive placebo.

Positive control: Where the subjects in control group receive other treatment or experimental intervention.

3. Randomization

Randomization means that every subject has an equal chance of being assigned to experimental or control group. This is also known as random assignment of subjects, which involves the placement of study subjects on a random basis.

Through random assignment of subject under experimental or control group, chances of systemic bias is eliminated.

True experimental design types

A. Classic randomized (Pretest-Posttest) control group design

This design is conducted as the following:

1. The researcher recruits a sample from the population.
2. A pre-intervention measures (the pre-test) is collected from the entire sample.
3. Subjects are then randomized to either the intervention or the control group .
4. After each group receives the experimental intervention or comparison/control
   intervention (usual care or standard treatment, education, or placebo),
5. Both groups complete post-intervention measures (the post-test) to see if any changes have occurred in the dependent variables.

Example

50 freshman students are randomly selected to participate in a tutorial study. Half are randomly assigned to a tutor for their first semester and half are not. All students are given a pretest at the beginning of the term and a posttest at the end of the term.

B. Posttest-only (After-Only Design) Control Group Design

This design is the less frequently used experimental design. This design is composed of two randomly assigned groups, but unlike the true experimental design, neither group is pretested or measured. The independent variable is introduced to the experimental group and not to the control group.

This design is conducted as the following:

1. This design does not involve any pre-measurement.
2. It is assumed that the two groups are similar in terms of pre-treatment measures on the dependent variable, because of the random assignment of test units to groups.
3. It involves only two groups and only one measurement per group.

Example

Students are randomly assigned to two groups of 50 each. The experimental (treatment) group receives a new teaching method during a special class session. The second group (control group) receives a traditional teaching method during a special lass session. No pretest is used for each group. Issues such as existing grades and other factors are examined as covariates.

C. Solomon Four-Group Design

This design has two groups that are identical to those used in the classic experimental design, plus two additional groups: an experimental after-group and a control after-group.

This design is conducted as the following:

1. The subjects were randomly assigned to one of four groups:

    i. Pretest, decision aid, immediate posttest

    ii. Pretest, no decision aid, immediate posttest

    iii. No pretest, decision aid, posttest

    iv. No pretest, no decision aid, posttest only

2. The study found no pretest sensitization, that knowledge increased significantly for those exposed to the decision aid, and that knowledge had some effect on conflict and anxiety.

➢ This design is used when it is suspected that, in taking a test more than once, earlier tests have an effect on later tests, for example, by learning or priming effects.

➢ In addition to the basic pretest, treatment and posttest design, do three additional tests, one without the treatment, one without the pretest and one without both pretest and treatment.

➢ This design contains two extra control groups, which serve to reduce the influence of confounding variables and allow the researcher to test whether the pretest itself has an effect on the subjects.

> In a test where there is no priming or learning effect, the pretest and scores without treatment will all be similar.

> When there is a priming or learning effect, then repeated tests without the treatment will show a significant change, while posttests without a pretest will give results dissimilar to the basic pretest and posttest.

Example (1)

100 freshman students are randomly selected to participate in a tutoring study. 25 are randomly assigned to a tutor for their first semester and given a pretest. 25 are randomly assigned to a group where no tutor is assigned and they are given a pretest. Another 25 are randomly assigned to a tutor but not given a pretest. The remaining 25 are randomly assigned to a group where no tutor is assigned and they have not given a pretest.

Example (2)

Rubel and colleagues (2010) used the Solomon four-group design to test the effects of exposure to a prostate cancer screening decision aid versus standard education in men age 50-70 years. They hypothesized that those who received the pretest would have higher posttest knowledge, decreased conflict, and decreased decisional anxiety

D. Randomized Block Design

This design is useful when there is only one major external variable that might influence the dependent variable.

This design is conducted as the following:

1. The test units are blocked or grouped on the basis of the external variable.
2. The researcher must be able to identify and measure the blocking variable.
3. By blocking the researcher ensures that the various experimental and control groups are matched closely on the external variable.

Example

In a study of college students, we might expect that students are relatively homogeneous with respect to class or year. So, we decide to block the sample into four groups: freshman, sophomore, junior, and senior. If our hunch is correct, that the variability within class is less than the variability for the entire sample, we will probably get more powerful estimates of the treatment effect within each block. Within each of our four blocks, we would implement the simple post-only randomized experiment.

E. Factorial Design

This design is used to measure the effects of two or more

independent variables at various levels. Unlike the randomized block design and the Latin square, factorial designs allow for interaction between variables. An interaction is said to take place when the simultaneous effect of two or more variables is different from the sum of their separate effects.

In a two-factor design, each level of one variable represents a row and each level of another variable represents a column. Multidimensional tables can be used for three or more factors.

It involves a cell for every possible combination of treatment variables.

Example

We would like to vary the amount of time the children receive instruction with one group getting 1 hour of instruction per week and another getting 4 hours per week. And, we would like to vary the setting with one group getting the instruction in-class and the other group being pulled-out of the classroom for instruction in another room. We could think about having four separate groups to do this, but when we are varying the amount of time in instruction, what setting would we use- in-class or pull-out. The two independent variables (setting and time of instruction) are the factors. Setting is factor A and time of instruction is factor B.

F. Cross over (A Repeated measures) design

In this design, subjects are exposed to all treatments but are randomly assigned to different orderings of treatments.

> ➤ The subjects serve as their own controls.
> ➤ When subjects are exposed to two different treatments or conditions, they may be influenced in the second condition by their experience in the first condition.

Example

Subject 1 first receives treatment A and then treatment B. Subject 2 might receive treatment B and then treatment A. A crossover design has the advantage of eliminating individual subject differences from the overall treatment effect, thus enhancing statistical power.

Strengths of true experimental design

The following are the strengths of true experimental design:

- The results of a true experimental design can be statistically analyzed and so there can be little argument about the results
- It is also much easier for other researchers to replicate the experiment and validate the results
- It is considered as the most powerful design to establish the causal relationship between independent and dependent variables
- In these studies, the controlled environment in which the

study is conducted can yield a greater degree, of purity in observation

- Conditions not found in a natural setting can be created in an experimental setting, where the independent variable is manipulated by investigator
- In the true experimental approach, we can often create conditions in a short period of time that may take years to occur naturally
- When an experiment is conducted in a laboratory, experimental unit or other specialized research setting, it is removed from the pressure and problems of real-life situations and the researcher can pursue his or her studies in a more leisurely, careful and concentrated way
- It has greater internal validity
- It uses fewer subjects.

Limitations of True Experimental Design

The following are some of the limitations of true experimental design:

- It is very difficult to get cooperation from the study participants and expensive to set up
- Most of the time, the results of experimental research designs
cannot be replicated in studies conducted on human beings

due to ethical problems

- In experimental studies conducted in natural settings like hospitals or community, it is not possible to impose control over extraneous variables
- There is no guarantee that a human or living organism will exhibit normal behavior under experimental conditions
- It can be too accurate and it is very difficult to obtain a complete rejection or acceptance of a hypothesis because the standards of proof required are so difficult to reach
- In a true experimental study, the study sample is kept small, there is a question as to how representative the findings of such studies can be
- It has les external validity
- It is not very practical.

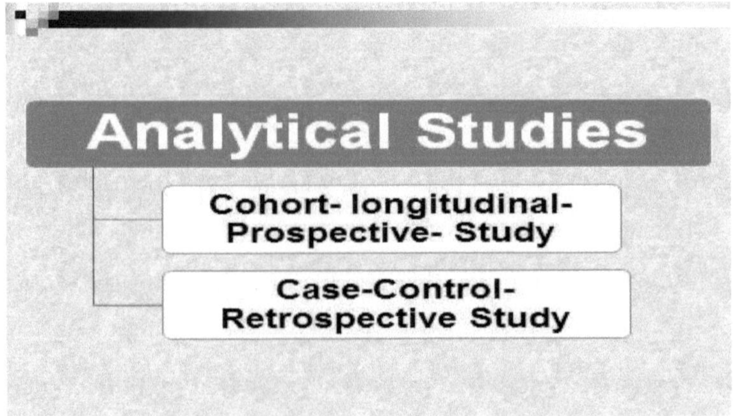

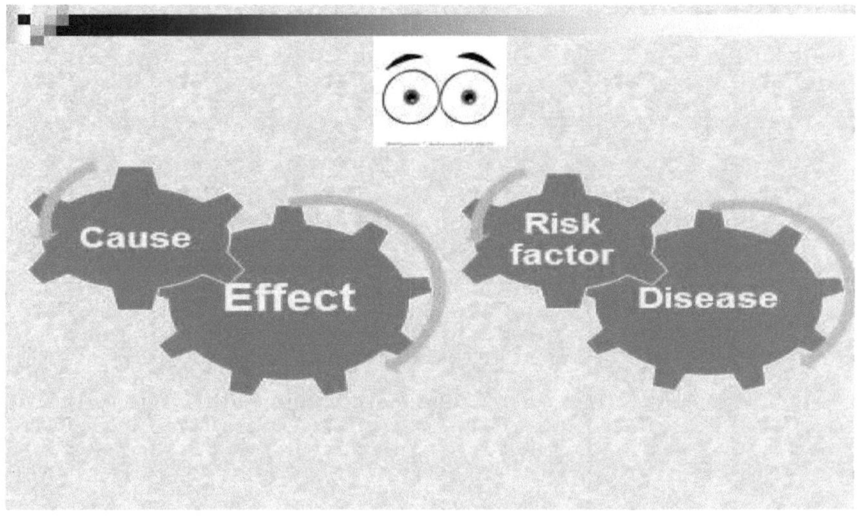

Whether <u>smoking</u> leads to <u>lung cane</u>?

OR

There is a relationship between <u>smoking</u> and <u>lung cane.</u>

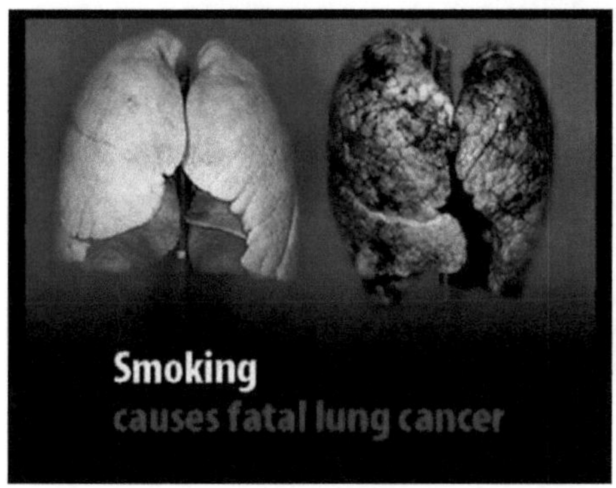

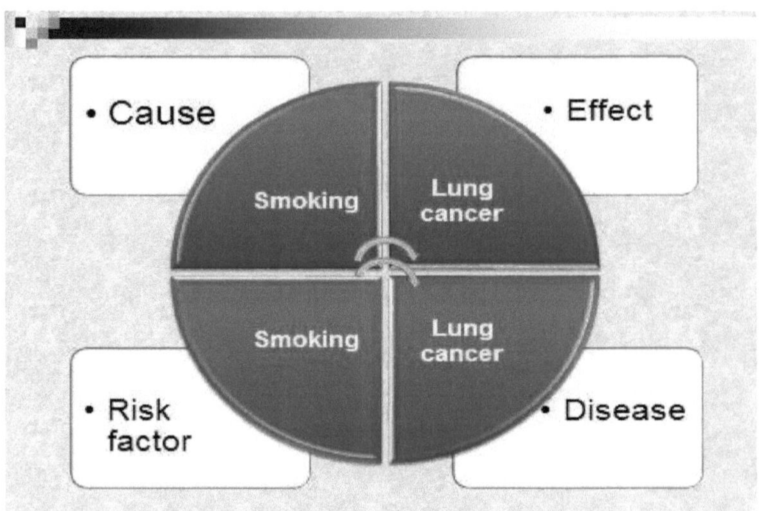

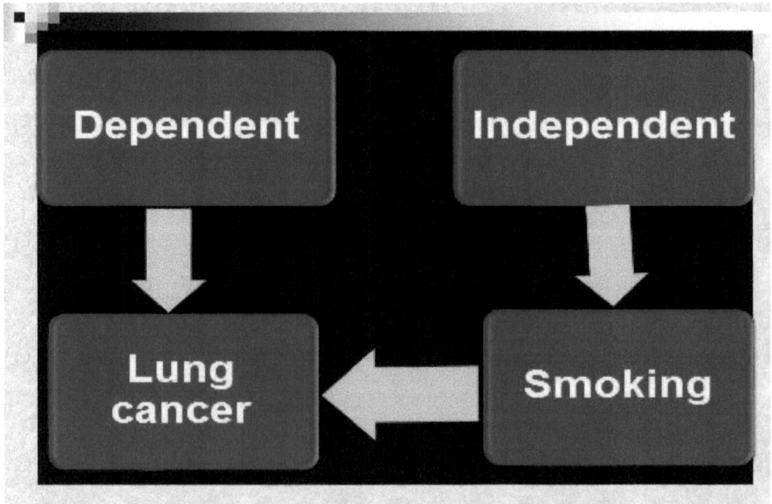

Analytical Studies

An analytical study is an observational study that describes associations and analyses them for possible cause and effect.

<table>
<tr>
<td>Cohort- longitudinal- Prospective Study</td>
<td></td>
</tr>
</table>

- The word cohort was the ancient Roman term for a group of soldiers who marched together into battle.
- The prospective cohort design is generally considered to be the "crème de la crème" of observational methodologies

In this method, investigator select a cohort i.e. a group of people of same age group and exposed to similar type of health risk (<u>cigarette smoking</u>) and a group of people of same age group but not exposed to health risk of <u>cigarette smoking</u>.

These two groups are followed for several years to find that how many people <u>of each</u> getting <u>cancer</u>.

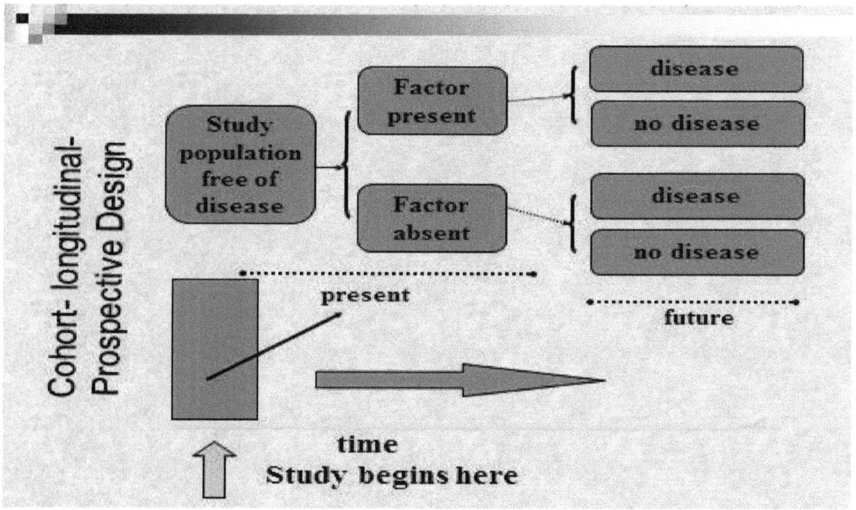

Case-Control- Retrospective Study

- A group of subjects who have a disease of interest (cases) and a group of patients without the disease (controls) are identified.
- Investigators then compare the extent to which each subject was previously exposed to the variable of interest, such as <u>a risk factor, a treatment </u>or <u>an intervention</u>.
- Case–control studies are useful for studying rare conditions and conditions with long intervals between exposure and outcome:

For example

Risk of developing cancer. In such situations, a prospective study will be difficult.

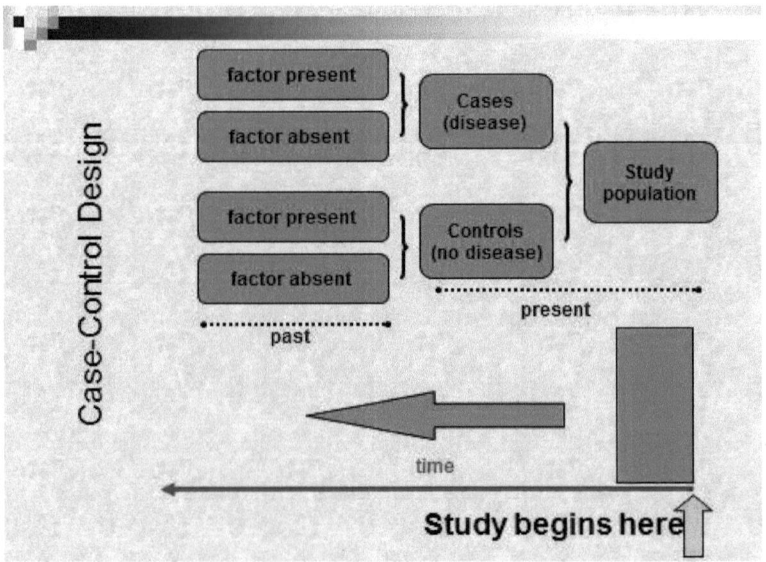

Comparison between Prospective and Retrospective design

Prospective	Retrospective
The investigators follow subjects for future events.	The investigators study present and past events.
Time–order relationships are clear (it is easy to decide that an outcome followed, rather than preceded, a possible cause).	You have difficulty in being sure which came first: the disease or the exposure.
Prospective is establishing causal sequence.	There is not strength of evidence as prospective study.
Estimate incidence	No estimation of incidence
Time and money consuming 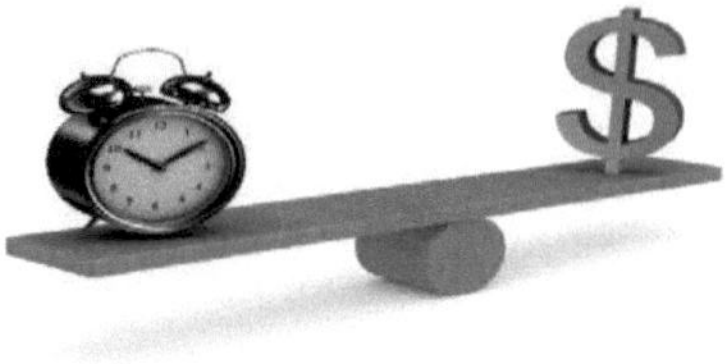	Easy to conduct and less expensive.
No recall of past events	Recall of past events (inaccurate).
This study is done on a group of people having similar characteristics e.g., age, sex, occupation and having equal suitability of the disease. 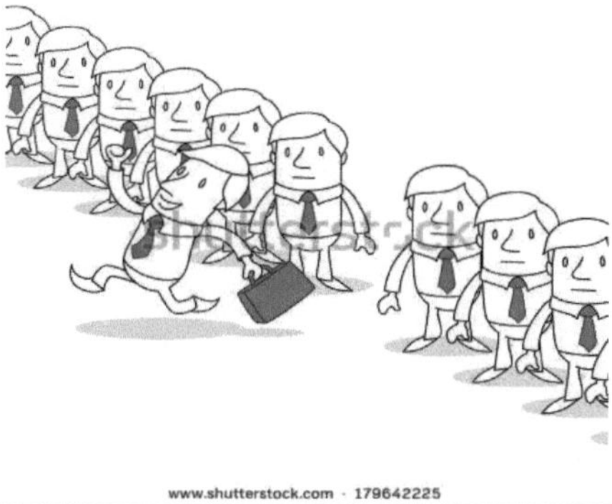 www.shutterstock.com · 179642225	A problem with case-control studies is that: Cases and controls may differ on a number of factors, (such as age, sex, or wealth) that you are not considering as potential causes. To ensure greater comparability between the two groups, and thereby avoid confounding, the controls could be matched for sex and age to the cases.

5.Data Collection

Definition of data collection

Data collection is the process of gathering and measuring information on targeted variables in an established systematic fashion, which then enables one to answer relevant questions and evaluate outcomes.

Consequences from improperly collected data include:

a) Inability to answer research questions accurately;

b) Inability to repeat and validate the study.

Plan for data collection

Importance of data collection plan

A plan for data collection should be developed so that:

- The researcher will have a clear overview of what tasks have to be carried out, who should perform them, and the duration of these tasks;
- The researcher can organize both human and material resources for data collection in the most efficient way; and
- The researcher can minimize errors and delays which may result from lack of planning (***For example***: The population not being available or data forms being misplaced).

Stages in the Data Collection Process

Three main stages can be distinguished:

Stage 1: Permission to proceed

Stage 2: Data collection

Stage 3: Data handling

Stage 1: Permission to proceed

Consent must be obtained from the relevant authorities, individuals and the community in which the project is to be carried out. This may involve organizing meetings at national or provincial level, at district and at village level.

For clinical studies this may also involve obtaining written informed consent.

Stage 2: Data collection

- Compilation and interpretation of primary and secondary sources of information.
- The integration of different sources will consolidate the write up of the report.

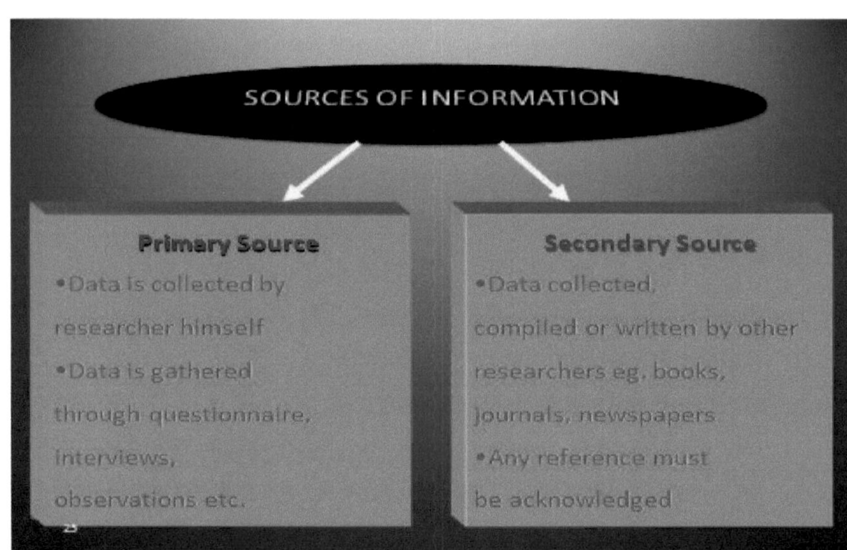

SOURCES OF INFORMATION
Primary Source
•Data is collected by researcher himself
•Data is gathered through questionnaire, interviews, observations etc.
Secondary Source
•Data collected, compiled or written by other researchers eg. books, journals, newspapers
•Any reference must be acknowledged

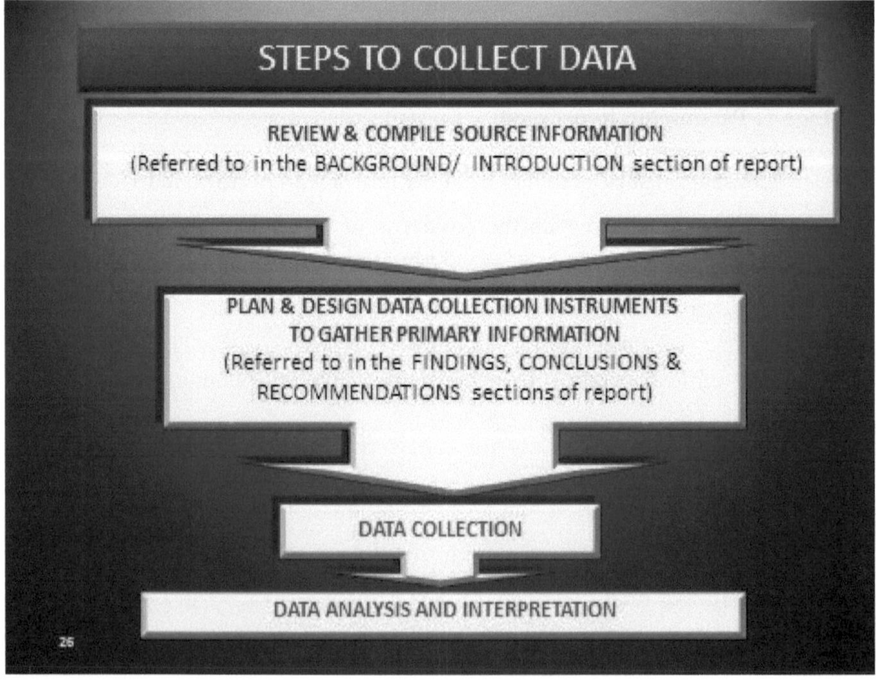

STEPS TO COLLECT DATA
REVIEW & COMPILE SOURCE INFORMATION
(Referred to in the BACKGROUND/ INTRODUCTION section of report)
PLAN & DESIGN DATA COLLECTION INSTRUMENTS TO GATHER PRIMARY INFORMATION
(Referred to in the FINDINGS, CONCLUSIONS & RECOMMENDATIONS sections of report)
DATA COLLECTION
DATA ANALYSIS AND INTERPRETATION

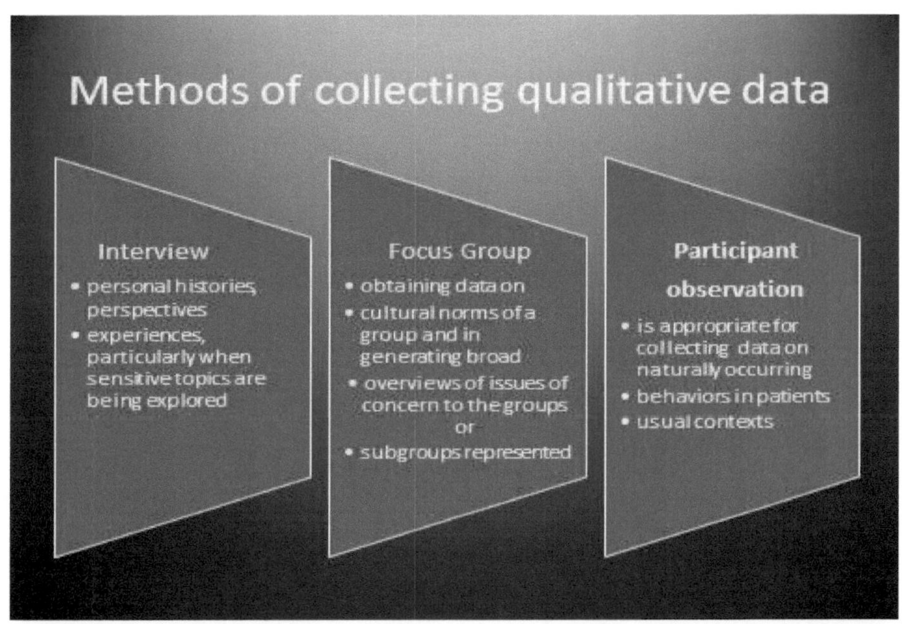

Methods of collecting qualitative data

Interview
• personal histories, perspectives
• experiences, particularly when sensitive topics are being explored

Focus Group
• obtaining data on
• cultural norms of a group and in generating broad
• overviews of issues of concern to the groups or
• subgroups represented

Participant observation
• is appropriate for collecting data on naturally occurring
• behaviors in patients
• usual contexts

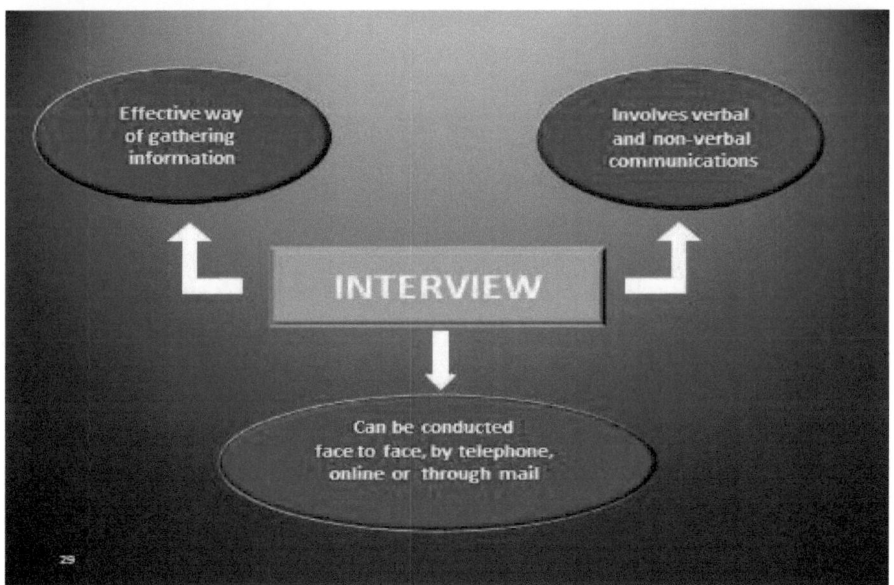

Effective way of gathering information

Involves verbal and non-verbal communications

INTERVIEW

Can be conducted face to face, by telephone, online or through mail

29

<u>Types of Interview</u>

1-Structured an interview/ quantitative interview

2-Semi -structured interviews

3- Unstructured interviews

<table>
<tr><td>**1.Structured   an   interview/ quantitative interview**</td><td></td></tr>
</table>

pre-planning of all the questions asked.

allow for exact replication of the interview with others.

conducted in various modes:

> $\Rightarrow$ face-to-face

> $\Rightarrow$ By telephone, videophone and internet Questionnaires and surveys are common

Examples of structured interview tools.

- Interviewer asking each respondent the same questions in the same way.

- A tightly structured schedule of questions is used, like a questionnaire

- For example: "Do you think that health services in this area are excellent, good, average or poor?

2-semi-structured interview

partial pre-planning of the questions.

allow for replication of the interview with others, but are less controlled.

Conducted in various modes

face-to-face, by telephone, videophone

but

face-to face is probably best.

Interviewer has a set of broad questions to ask and may also have some prompts to help the interviewee **But** the interviewer has the time and space to respond to the interviewees responses

3-Unstructured or depth or in depth

The interviewer goes into the interview with the aim of discussing a limited number of topics

frames the questions on the basis of the interviewee's previous response.

one or two topics are discussed they are covered in great detail.

E.g, the interviewer saying:

- "I'd like to hear your views on the GP role in PCTs".

Subsequent questions would depend on how the interviewee respond

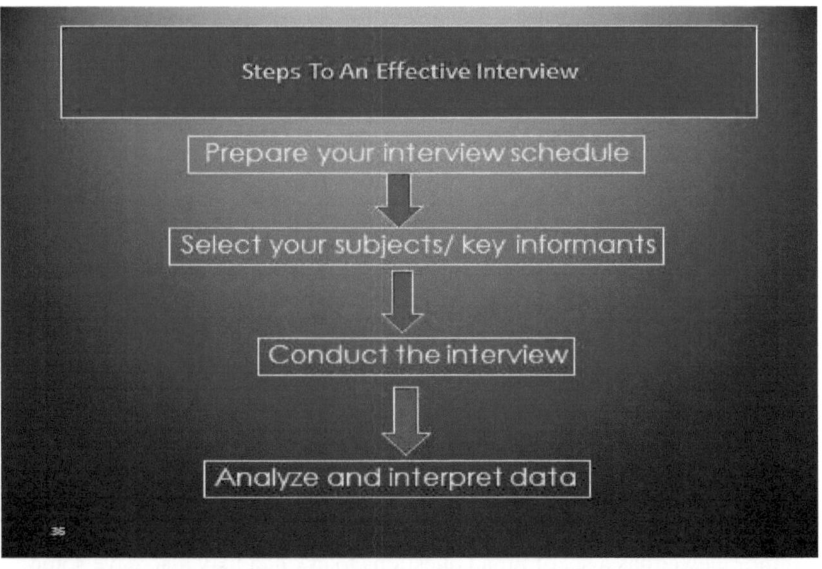

Steps To An Effective Interview
Prepare your interview schedule
Select your subjects/ key informants
Conduct the interview
Analyze and interpret data

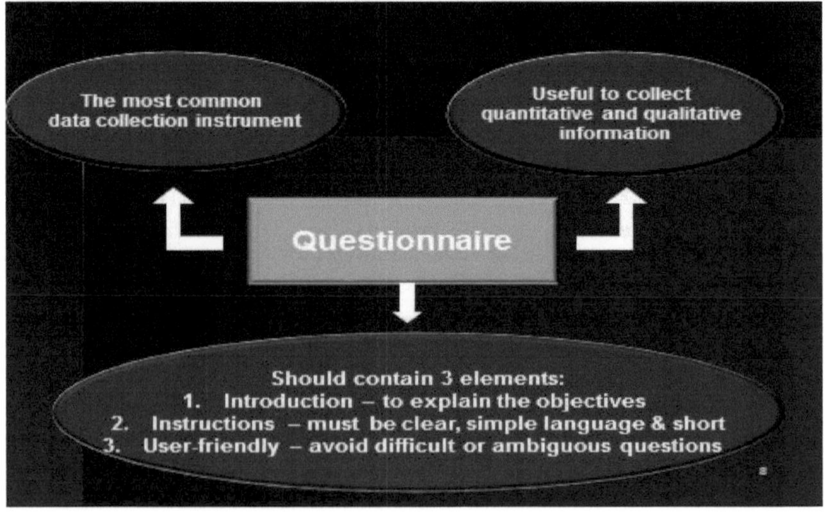

The most common data collection instrument
Useful to collect quantitative and qualitative information
Questionnaire
Should contain 3 elements:
1. Introduction – to explain the objectives
2. Instructions – must be clear, simple language & short
3. User-friendly – avoid difficult or ambiguous questions

A questionnaire is a research instrument consisting of a list of questions with: Instructions on how to record the answers. (self a dministered and is mostly quantitative)

A questionnaire should meet at least five general objectives

Each question should be:

1- Interpreted by different respondents in the same way and in a way that is consistent with what the investigator expected.
2- Specify the type of answer expected.
3- Ask something all respondents are able to provide.
4- Ask something all respondents are willing to provide.
5- Each question should be administered to respondents in the same way

<u>Question warding</u>

1-Keep question short

2-Avoid leading question

3-Avoid double barreled questions

4-Avoid Hypothetical question

5-Questions about other people

6-Questions which can be obtained more easily from other recourses

7-Slang

8-Questions which depends on the memory of respondents

9-Avoid negative phrasing

Example 1. Open Format Questions

Q 1. What is your date of birth? |__|__| |__|__| |__|__|__|__| month day year

Q2. In the *3 months before you got pregnant, how many cigarettes or packs of cigarettes did you smoke on an average day? (A pack has 20 cigarettes.)*

____Cigarettes OR ____ Packs

Example: Open Format Questions of a Sensitive Nature

Q 3-. In the *3 months before you got pregnant, how many times did you drink 5 alcoholic drinks or more in one sitting?*

____Times

⇒ Closed ended question

Dichotomous question:

yes/no, true/false, agree/disagree

Do you agree for this medication?

Agree

Disagree

Are you suffering from headache?

Yes

No

⇒ Multiple choice question

Multiple response:
What sources do you use for writing term reports? (check all that apply)
Single response:
How many hours do you exercise per week (check only one response)

Examples:

Which of the following outdoor activities did you do last week?

- Running

- Walking

- Hiking

- Cycling

- Swimming

⇒ **Likert-type Scale:**

Each response is assigned a numeric ranking based on a continuum that contains predetermined units of measurement

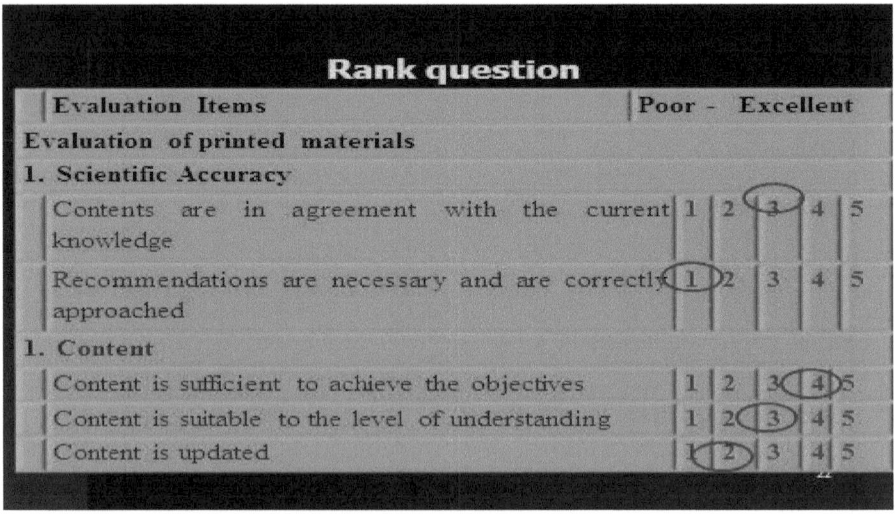

Rank question					
Evaluation Items	Poor - Excellent				
Evaluation of printed materials					
1. Scientific Accuracy					
Contents are in agreement with the current knowledge	1	2	③	4	5
Recommendations are necessary and are correctly approached	①	2	3	4	5
1. Content					
Content is sufficient to achieve the objectives	1	2	3	④	5
Content is suitable to the level of understanding	1	2	③	4	5
Content is updated	1	②	3	4	5

Did you do use sunscreen during the following outdoor activities during the past six months?

Always Sometimes Seldom   Never

Running

Walking

Cycling

Scales for measuring attitude (Lickert)

Stray dogs carry a higher risk of rabies

No, I strongly disagree

No, I disagree quite a lot

No, I disagree just a little

I'm not sure about this

Yes, I agree just a little

Yes, I agree quite a lot

Yes, I strongly agree

Focus Group
Discussion (FGD)

- Another unstructured group meeting conducted by a manager or a consultant.
- A small group of 8-10 people is selected representing a larger group of people
- Type of qualitative research where small homogenous groups of people are brought together to informally discuss specific topics under the guidance of a moderator
- Purpose: to identify issues and themes, not just interesting information, and not "counts"
- Type of qualitative research where small homogenous groups of people are brought together to informally discuss specific topics under the guidance of a moderator
- Purpose: to identify issues and themes, not just interesting information, and not "counts"

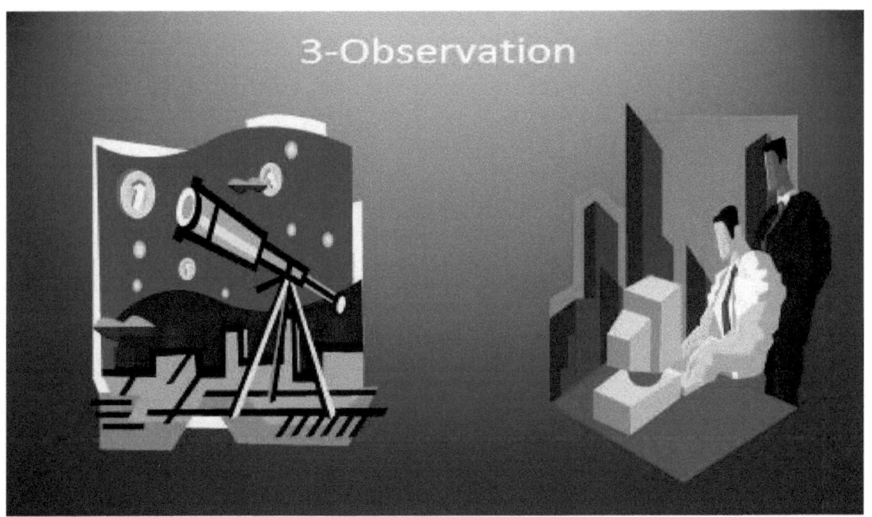

* Observation is the action or process of closely observing or monitoring and the ability to notice significant details.
* The researcher through observation watching, listening and recording phenomena systematically.

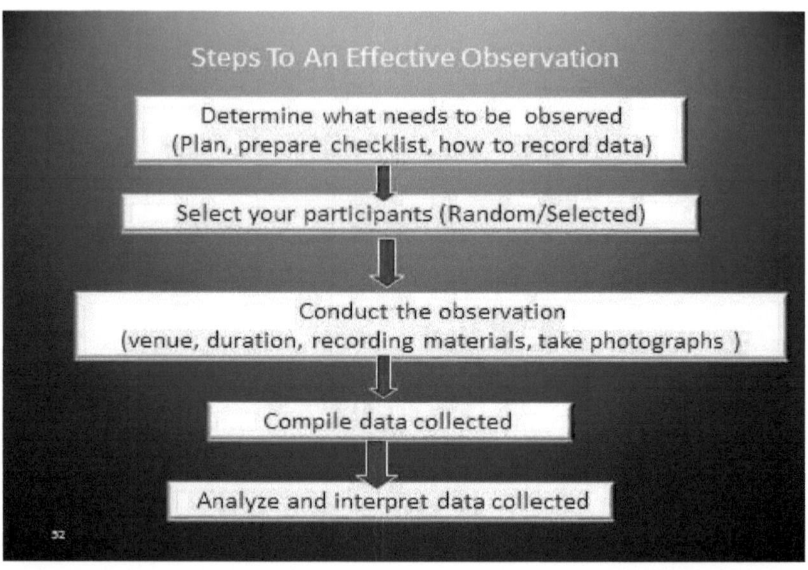

Example of checklist:

Infection Control Auditing Tool

Items	Yes = 1	No= 0	Comments
There is infection control team			
Nurses are trained on infection control			
Doctors are trained on infection control			
There is a plan for infection control training			Specify schedule
Staff know where to access infection control consultation			
Nurses are vaccinated with all doses of hepatitis B vaccine			
Doctors are vaccinated with all doses of hepatitis B vaccine			
Hand washing			
Bar soap present at available sink			
Sinks are available for hand washing			
Liquid antiseptic soap available			
List the available antiseptic solution			

Stage 3: Data handling

Once the data have been collected and checked for completeness and accuracy, a clear procedure should be developed for handling and storing them. Decide if the questionnaires are to be numbered; identify the person who will be responsible for storing the data; and how they are going to be stored.

Source of Information

From where or from whom will you get the information?

- Existing information – records, reports, program documents, logs, journals
- People – participants, parents, volunteers, teachers
- Pictorial records and observations – video or photos, observations of events, artwork

<u>Sampling Concepts</u>

<u>Sample and population;</u>

<u>Population;</u> is an entire set of subjects, objectives, events or elements being studied. <u>Example;</u> individuals, medical records, diagnosis,.etc. researchers may be interested in describing the characteristics of private versus public institutions in different geographic locations. Type of institutions and geographic areas would be the units that define the population.

Sample It is not feasible to study everybody in particular population, so is selected. If the sample represents the total population, the study results can be generalized to include the entire population and settings being studied.

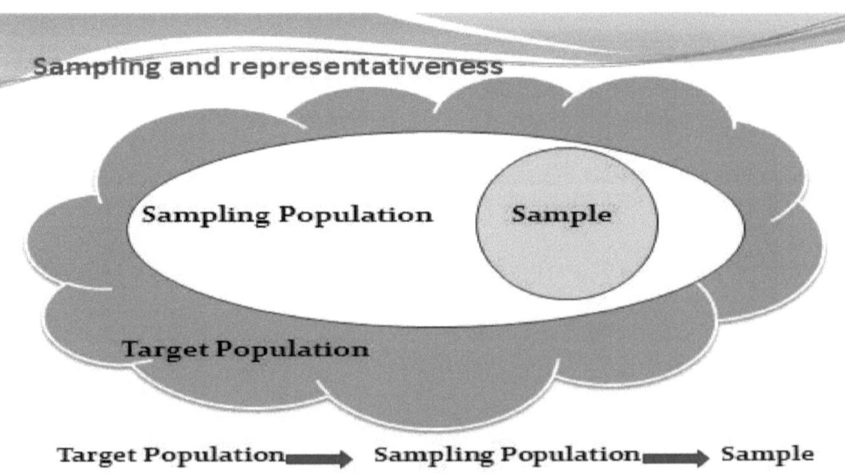

Target population; the entire set of elements about which the researcher would like to make generalizations. If a researcher studies people with type 2 diabetes so the target population is all people with type 2 diabetes.

If sample come from some portions of the target population so it called **Accessible population;** that is readily available to researcher and represents the target population as closely as possible as type 2 diabetes from several community hospitals, home care services, large academic health science center.

<u>Sampling</u> = is the process of selecting individuals for a study in a way that individual represent the larger group from which they were selected .

Probability or Nonprobability are both appropriate, based on how the problem is conceptualized and according to the method used to achieve Representation

<u>**Types of Sampling**</u>

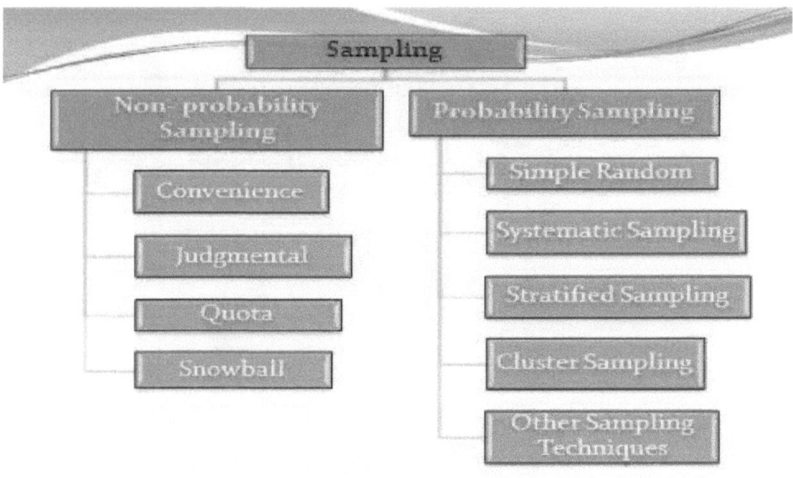

Probability Sample	Nonprobability Sample
Every subject or element has an equal chance of being chosen	Sample not selected randomly so the degree to which the sample represent the population is unknown

Simple random sample
2- Stratified random sample
    * Proportional
    * Disproportional
3- Custer sample
4- Systematic sample
	1- convenience (accidental)
	    * Snowball
	    * Network
	2- Quota Sample
	3- Purposive Sample

A- Probability Sampling

1- Simple Random Sample:

- Every subject has an equal and independent chance of being chosen. It only considered to represent the target population.

- No sampling technique guarantees a representative sample.
  Example: 40 patients experiencing supraventricular
  tachycardia (SVT) were randomly selected from a list of
  medical records department.
  Whenever the researcher use the phrase random = simple
  random sample

True random sampling; it defines the population and identifying a
  Sampling Frame.

A Sampling Frame; it is a list of all subjects or elements in the
  population.

How conduct random selection?

1- Blindly selection; write each individual's name or element and put
   into container and select blindly until you get the desired number
   for the study.

2- The table of random numbers; it contains thousands of digits (0 to
   9) with no systematic order or relationship. It consists of 3 to 5
   digits.

**Steps that should be follow to use the random table to select the
random numbers;**

1. Identify the population.
2. Determine the desired sample size.
3. List all members of the accessible population.
4. Assign all individuals on the list a consecutive number from one to
   the required number.

5. Select an arbitrary number in the table (just close your eyes and point to one). From that point read consecutive numbers in any direction (horizontal) or (vertically).
6. If the number chosen corresponds to that assigned to any of the individuals in the population, then that individual is in the sample.

Example; if the population 800 and number selected was 375, the individual assigned number 375 would be in the sample. If the population is only 300 member so individual number 375 would be ignored.

7. Go to the next number in the column and repeat step 6 until the desired number of individuals have been selected for the sample.

Simple Random Sample

Advantages;

- The appropriate, sample representation in relation to the population is maximized.

Disadvantages

- Time consuming Impossible to obtain an accurate or complete listing Time frame

Random Selection versus Random Assignment

Random Selection	Random Assignment
<ul><li>How the individuals may be chosen to participate in a study</li><li>It is not prerequisite for random assignment</li></ul>	<ul><li>It is the random allocation of subjects to either an experimental or control group.</li></ul>

2- Stratified Random Sampling:

It is a process of selecting a sample to identify sub groups (or strata) in the population that are represented in the sample. Example; population can be stratified according to age, gender (sex), ethnicity (different races, cultures, customs, ..etc), socioeconomic status, diagnosis, type of care, type of institution, geographical location and so on.

3- Cluster Sampling;

It is group not individuals, are randomly selected. It is used for convenience when the population is very large or spread over a wide geographic area.

3- Systematic Sampling:

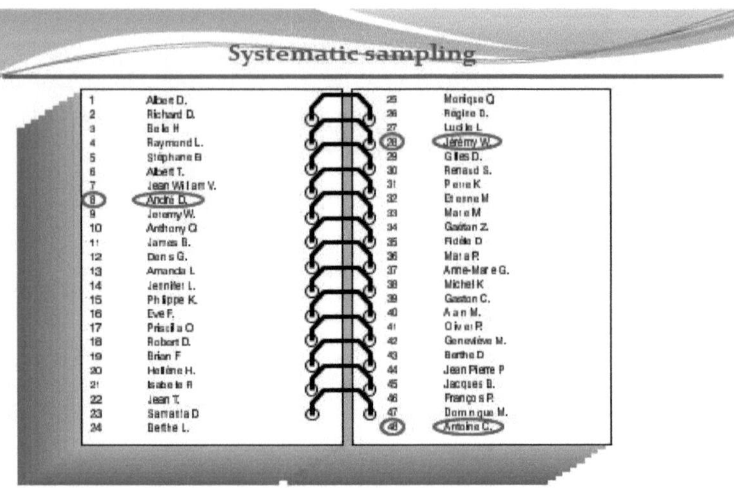

Individuals or elements of the population are selected from a list by taking every kth individual (k=sampling interval) depends on the size of the list and desired sample size. It differ than the other sampling as all members of the population do not have a chance of being selected for the sample.

Example;

To select 250 patients from a population list of 1000 patients, divide 1000 by 250 to determine the size of the sampling interval. If k =4, selection involves taking every fourth name

A major advantage of systematic sampling is that data are collected more conveniently and efficiently.

B- No probability Sampling

Many nursing research studies use no probability sampling because of the difficulties in obtaining random access to population. It is more feasible to obtain but cannot generalize the finding, as the sample chosen may not represent the larger population.

1- Convenience Sampling: (accidental)

It is the collection of data from subjects or objects available or accessible to the researcher. It does not use random selection. Data collected from the available subjects and meet the criteria.

- Advantage;

    1- easy in carrying out the research.

    2- saving time and money.

- Disadvantage;

    1- potential for sampling bias.

    2- use sample that may not represent population

    4- limited ability for result to be generalized.

2- Snowball Sampling: (network sampling)

It is useful in studies specify certain trait that is ordinarily difficult to find. It relies on previously identified members of a group to identify other members of population. When the researcher has found a few subjects with the needed criteria, these individuals are asked to help the researcher get in touch with others having similar characteristics.

Advantage;   1- social network

2- subjects may be friends have common characteristics.

Disadvantage; 1- biases because subjects are not independent of each other's as they volunteer to participate.

Example; it is used in qualitative study as, caregivers of elderly parents, than they inform others they know in the same situation.

Nurses volunteered to participate in a study to discuss the knowledge and expertise in one of nursing experience. Some nurses participated after hearing about the study through colleagues (network sampling)

3- Quota Sampling;

It identifies the strata (social level) of the population based on specific characteristics. It differs from stratified random sampling in that the subjects are not randomly selected for each stratum. The quota is computed proportionally (part of share) or disproportionally.

Example; select quota sampling for families expecting a first baby and families expecting a second baby. It expecting to get it from one site as public health prenatal clinic or from community sources as Lamaze classes. This process was followed for families expecting a second baby too.

4- Purposive Sampling: (judgmental or theoretical)

It is commonly used in qualitative research. The researcher selects certain cases to be in the study (Hand-picks). Those selected cases are thought to best represent the phenomenon being studied and to be typical of the population. The researcher makes a judgment regarding the type of subjects needed to provide the most useful information about the studied phenomenon.

Advantage; hand-pick of the sample by researcher

Disadvantage; sampling bias

Example; studies women who were directly at risk of AIDS

Adequacy of the Sample

Sample Size;

There are no hard and fast rules about sample size. In quantitative studies,

The purpose is to explore meanings and phenomena; an adequate sample size in these types of studies is to be large enough to accomplish its goal.

Example; study the implications of migration on emotional status or women were interviewed who were at risk for AIDS because of injection drug use or because they were heterosexual partners of injection drug users.

In both examples; the exact number of subjects was not determined in advance.

- In quantitative studies, sample size is linked to data collection and type of analysis.

- A study of large number sample is not more valid than studies of smaller sample sizes. **_So researcher need to considered the following criteria when evaluating the adequacy of the sample;**

1. Purpose of the study.
2. Research design
3. Sampling method
4. Data analysis.
5. Use formula of power analysis

To critical questions for determining adequacy of a sample include:

A- How representative is the sample relative to target population?

B- To whom dose the researcher wish to generalize the results of the study?

Criteria of Adequate sampling: The object of sampling is to have a Sample as representative as possible with little sampling error as possible.

Facts about the study sampling:

- Every study will contain some error; results will never be 100% representative of the population.

- Sampling that is biased or too small, however, threatens the external validity of the design.

External Validity: It is the extent to which study results can be generalized from the study sample to other subjects, populations, measuring instruments, and settings. Threats to the ability to generalize the findings are in terms of study design, include the following;

. Interaction of selection & treatment; if sample confined to certain criteria we cannot generalize it to whom do not have such criteria.

. Interaction of setting and treatment; bias exists when member of different settings participate in studies.

. Interaction of treatment and history; this threat to external validity concerns the ability to generalize results of different periods of time in the past or future. As diet researches now differed than 20 years ago.

Ethics in Research

Outline

- Definition of research ethics.
- Components of research ethics.
- Principle of research ethics.
- Component of an ethically valid
- Informed consent.
- Vulnerable groups.
- Research Ethics Committees

Introduction

Ethics in research is concerned with value judgments and in particular with value judgments about right or wrong, good or bad behavior.It important to understand however, that ethics is not just about identifying or ascribing the values of good or bad or right or wrong to certain people, decision, and action, Anther critical role of ethics is to provide sound justification for the value judgments we make.

Definition:-

Involves application of fundamental ethical principle to the variety of topics involving scientific research.

Ethical consideration throughout research process

1) Criteria for a good research topic.
2) Ethics in research design.
3) Ethical ethics in implementation of the study.

*Principle of Research Ethics:-

There are three Ethical principles

1-Respect:

This principle cited by influential Belmont report is autonomy which refers to obligation on the part of the investigator to respect each participant as person capable of making informed decision regarding participation in the research study.

The first principle which includes:-

A-Right to full disclosure.

The nature of the study, the risk, the benefits and alternatives with an extended opportunity to ask question the principle of autonomy finds expression in the informed consent documents

B-Right to self –determination.

The principle to self determination means that prospective participant have the right to decide voluntarily whether to participate in the study without the risk of any penalties prejudicial.

2-Beneficence

It is the second ethical principle which refers to the obligation on the part of investigator to attempt to maximize benefit for the individual participant and the society.

Beneficence that the principle that contains multiple dimensions:-

A-Freedom from harm.

Although, protecting study participant from physical harm is in study may be subtle and thus require closer attention and sensitivity.

B-Freedom from exploitation.

Shouldn't place participant at the disadvantage or expose them to situation for which they haven't been explicitly

For example, person describing his economic circumstances to a researcher shouldn't be exposed to the risk of losing Medicaid benefits, the person reporting drug abuse shouldn't fear exposure to criminal authorities.

3-Justice.

It is the third ethical principle invoked in research with human subject which equitable selection of participant s.

For example, avoiding participant population that may be un fairly coerced into participating such as institutionalized children

The principle of justice also requires equality in distribution of benefits and burden among population groups likely benefits from research.

*Components of an ethically valid informed consent:-

1-Disclosure:-

The potential participant must be informed as fully as of the nature and purpose of the research, the procedure to be used, the expected benefits to the participant or society the informed consent document must also disclose what compensation and medical treatment are available in the case of research the document should make it clear whom to contact with question about research study

2-Understanding

The participant must understand what has explained and must be given the opportunity to ask question and have answered by one of the investigator the informed consent document must be written in lay language, avoiding technical jargon

3-Voluntariness:-

The participant consent to participate in the research must be voluntary, free of any coercion or promises of benefits unlikely to participation.

4-Competence:-

The participant must be competent to give consent. if the participant is not competent due to mental status, disease or emergency, a designated surrogate may provide consent if it is in the participants best interests to participate in certain emergency.

******

<u>Vulnerable groups</u>

Definition:-

(The term used in federal guidelines) may be incapable of giving fully informed consent (mentally retarded people) or may be high risk of unintended side effects because of their circumstances as pregnant women

Among the groups that nurse researcher should consider as being especially vulnerable are the following:-
   1- Children as (students and institutionalized children).
   2- Mentally disabled people.
   3- Physically disabled people.
   4- Pregnant women.

1-Childern:-
   Legally and ethically, children don't have the competence to give their informed consent if the child is developmentally mature enough to understand the basic information (12year-old child)

2- Mentally disabled people:-
   People whose disability makes it impossible for them to weigh the risks and benefits of participation
(e.g. people affected by mental retardation, mental illness, and unconsciousness) in such cases, the researcher generally obtains the written consent of the persons legal guardian.

3-Physicaly disabled people:-
for certain physical disabilities, special procedures obtaining consent may be required

For example, with deaf people, the entire consent process may need to in writing for people who have physical impairment preventing them from writing (or for people who cannot read or write) alternatives procedure for documenting informed consent such as audio taping or videotaping the consent proceeding can be used.

<u>Research Ethics Committees</u>

The (state name of Faculty or Institution) is committed to high quality research on all aspects of the health and behavior of people, and such research is possible only through the participation of humans subjects in research.

Goals of REC.
1) Is to enhance the well-being of society.
2) An important objective of research involving human subjects is protection of the rights and welfare of subjects who participate in research.
3) help to ensure the dignity, safety of subjects who participate in research.

Principles of REC include;
Ethical principle includes:
1. Autonomy (respect for persons).
2. Beneficence (protecting subject walfare).
3. Non maleficence (minimizing potential harms of research).
4. Justice (avoidance of exploitation).
5. Other five domains include.
6. Ethics
7. Science
8. information
9. health and safety
10. financial and intellectual property

Constitution of the REC.

(A) Chairperson:

- Member with experience in research ethics.
- Qualifications of the chair;
- Aperson on the academic staff
- Reasonable experience in performing research.
- Basic training in research ethics.
- Reasonable communication skills and leadership characteristic.

Responsibilities:

The chair person responsible for the action of the REC Include:

1) Scheduling of regular meetings.
2) Communication between the REC, member of the research staff.
3) Orientation and Training of REC member.
4) REC Research Review Evaluations procedures, criteria, and actions.
5) Meeting frequency.
6) Quorum Requirements
7) Voting and Decision Making
8) Follow-up.

REC Meeting;

- Attendance at the meeting.
- Date and time of meeting.
- Names of members present.
- Names of member absent.
- Names of investigator present.

<u>**Role of Research Ethics Committees.**</u>

1) The REC shall review and have authority to approve, require modifications in (to secure approval) or disapprove initial and continuing reviews of all research activities.

2) The REC must report to the (Dean or President) unanticipated problems involving risks to subject.

3) REC must advise investigators in designing research projects in a manner to minimize potential harm to human subjects.

4) Approve research that meet established criteria for protection of human subjects.

5) Monitor approved research to ascertain that human subjects protect.

6) Analysis of risks and benefits; the REC will identify all risks (psychological, physical, social, and economic) involving in research.

7) Privacy of subjects and confidentiality procedure to protect subjects data; REC ensure the confidentiality of data obtain from the subjects.

Communicating research finding

<u>*Out line*</u>

1- Definition of communication

2- Benefits of communicating research finding.

3- The major part of research articles

- Title page
- Introduction
- Research question and hypothesis
- Method
- Results
- Discussion, conclusion,
- Appendices
- Reference

4- Methods of communicating research finding

5- APA style

<u>*Communicating Research Results*</u>

"......... communication truly occurs only when the message desired to be sent by the speaker or writer is received by the intended audience.

<u>*Benefits*</u>

1- Increases external validity

2- Access to unique samples

3- Ads unique perspectives

4- Facilitates grant applications

5- More relevant

it benefits to the following

1- Institutional

2- The research community

3- Societal

4- Personal

1- Institutional

1- Raises the University's research profile.

2- Assists in Our gouvernement relations (subsidies, scholarships, Grants)

3- Serves as a recruitment tool

4- Assists in Our fundraising efforts

2- Societal

1- Improve existing conditions

2- Educate

3- Set new challenges

4- Provoke debate

5- Serve as an inspiration

3-Personal

1- Raises your personal research profile

2- Opens up a new forum to explain your research

3- Lets you share your professional expertise

4- Could lead to other arrangements/opportunities

Methods of communicating research finding

1- Magazine

2- Newspaper

3- Informational Web Page (Wikipedia, Encyclopedia Web sites)

4- Professional paper from Internet

5- Videotape

6- Article Index

7- General Book

8- Popular Pamphlet

9- Bibliography

10- Journal Article

11- Dissertation

12- Electronic sources

Research process and research report

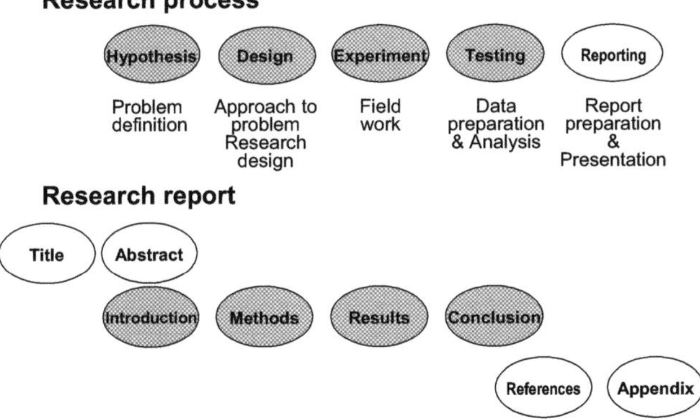

The Major Parts of a Research Article

1- title page

2- Introduction

3- Review of the Literature

4- Research Questions and/or Hypotheses

5- Methods

6- Results

7- Discussion

8- Appendices

9- References and Notes

1-_title page_

2-Abstract

- Brief comprehensive summary
- 75-120 words
- Concise
- Self-contained
- Non evaluative
- Coherent
- Readable
- One paragraph
- Highly succinct
- Is not an introduction
- 1st section to be read, therefore important
- This is one of the most difficult parts of a report to write. It should give your reader a brief but complete summary or overview of the entire report from aims to conclusions
- From the abstract alone, your reader should know what you have done and found out
- It is the last thing that you write
- What your research aim was.
- Key background theory.
- What data were collected from whom, and how.
- How it was analysed.
- Key findings.

3-INTRODUCTION

- WHAT you have done – aims/objectives.
- WHY you have done it – justification.
- HOW you have presented the report – structure/ signposting.
- This sets the scene for the report, by introducing & explaining information needed to understand the rest of the report.
- You'll put your reading here. It gives:
- brief background to the study
- explains reason[s] for the work carried out
- Explains connections with previous work i.e. reviewing relevant technical papers (referencing!)
  This is the section where you will bring in any reading & cite the work you've read
- At the end of the introduction
- explain your aims clearly
- introduce how you will address these
- explain briefly how the report is structured [signposting]; helpful/reader- friendly
- it start from general knowledge to specific

4-METHODOLOGY

- Information needs.
- Research design.
- Research strategy.
- Methods.
- Sample.
- Procedure.
- Analysis.
- Is it repeatable to the reader?

- Have you explained the rationale behind your chosen means of collecting information?
- Are your research methods the most appropriate given your chosen hypothesis or research question, and your subsidiary questions or objectives?
- Are you making assumptions? You know what you did in terms of research methods – have you expressed yourself clearly and given adequate details? Would someone else be able to replicate your study on the basis of the information you have given?
- Any limitations? Anything you might have done differently?
- The aim of this section is to enable another researcher to repeat your methods so you need to explain to the reader
- How you designed the model
- Reasons for choices made etc.
- Certain functions of a software package you have used This section should also demonstrate that you are using standard technical procedures

5-RESULTS

- There is no one correct way to present your results. Some ways could be:
-
- Address each of your hypotheses, research questions.
- By independent and dependent variable.
- By research method.
- Graphs **only** if they add to understanding.
- Use quotes sparingly for qualitative data.
- Only report relevant results.

- Presents the data or results i.e. data from the simulation/ model or experiment. There is little analysis here, unless you have a combined results & discussion chapter
- **You need to consider the most appropriate method of organising & presenting results**
- Do not just include figures & tables, ensure that
- the text provides:
- a commentary guiding the reader through the figures & tables
- references to all of these

6-Discussion

- In this section you interpret your data or results, in other words analysing your results & discussing the main findings of your lab work or simulation
- Keep your project aims in mind- don't deviate from these.
- If there are any limitations of your study, state them.
- Broaden the scope of your discussion to compare your findings with those of earlier work i.e. link back to to earlier sections

7-Conclusions

- This section is short & succinct
- State what you major conclusions are, referring back to your original aims. Have you achieved these aims?
- Highlight key features
- Discuss what advances you have made
- Some reports also include a Further Work or Recommendations section

8-Appendices

- To make your report easy to read & not swamp your reader with too much data, it is often useful to include some material e.g. code, full programmes in an appendix (cd or paper?)

- Many readers of your report may not read these sections & certainly should not need to read them to follow your report.

- However, some readers will want to analyse your detailed results in greater depth e.g. to compare with their own findings.

- If you include any appendices, then reference them in the main report (otherwise the reader will not be aware of them or fail to understand their purpose).

- The presentation of appendices needs to be of the same standard as the body of the report. Each appendix needs a self-explanatory title.

- Examples of what should be contained in the Appendices:

- Listing of code developed

- Scripts

- Interviews

- Story boards

- An Appendix may be on paper or on media such as a CD (check with your supervisor)

- Do not put something in an Appendix that the reader of your dissertation requires to follow your work

- Appendices should be numbered in a similar manner to the dissertation sections but beginning with a letter, e.g.

  Appendix A.1

  Appendix B.2.1

  Appendix C

9-REFERENCES

- Include author's name, complete title of the cited work, title of the source, volume, issue, year of publication, and pages cited.
- What is the purpose of including APA-style references in the body of a paper?
- The references in the body of your paper give appropriate credit to the person or persons whose <u>words</u> or <u>ideas</u> you are using to <u>support</u> what you have written in your paper. If you do not give credit to those whose work you use, you are guilty of <u>plagiarism,</u> which is a **<u>VERY serious violation of academic integrity</u>**.
- **Reference List – General Guidelines**
- On a separate page
- References (the title) is centered on top line
- Alphabetical list of works cited
- If same author cited more than once, chronologically listed
- Double spaced
- Hanging indent
- Titles of works and volume number in italics

- ***<u>what is the APA Style?</u>***
- Publication Manual of the American Psychological Association
- In 1929, the APA published a manual with instructions for authors on how to prepare manuscripts for publication in psychology journals
- Later used for theses, term papers, etc.
- Latest edition 5th in 2001
- Widely used in the social sciences
- **Parenthetical (Within-Text) Citations**
- Author's(s') last name
- Year of publication

- Page number (if quoting)
- Example:

  (Kosik, 1999, p. 17)

  Book with one author

  Carter, R. (1998). *Mapping the mind.*

  > Berkeley, CA: University of

- California Press
- **Multiple Authors**
- 2 authors – cite both names separated by & Example: (Kosik & Martin, 1999, p. 127)

Book with two authors

Struck, W., Jr., & White, E. B. (1979).

> *The elements of style* (3rd ed.).

- New York: Macmillan
- 3-5 authors – cite all authors first time; after first time, use et al. Example:

  (Wilson et al., 2000)

6 or more authors – cite first author's name and et al.

Example:

(Perez et al., 1992) Book with six or more authors

Wolchik, S. A., West, S. G., Sandler, I. N.,

> Tein, J., Coatsworth, D., Lengua, L.,

> et al. (2000). An experimental

> evaluation of…

Book with no author

Merriam-Webster's collegiate dictionary

> (10th ed.). (1993). Springfield, MA:

> Merriam-Webster.

Book with editors

Allison, M. T., & Schneider, I. E. (Eds.).

(2000). *Diversity and the recreation profession: Organizational perspectives*. State College, PA: Venture.

Chapter in Book

Stern, J. A., & Dunham, D. N. (1990).

The ocular system. In J. T. Cacioppo & L. G. Tassinary (Eds.), *Principles of psychophysiology: Physical, social, and inferential elements* (pp. 513-553). Berkeley, CA: University of California Press.

Article in press

Jones, R. (in press). The new healthcare lexicon. *Journal of Health.*

- **Multiple Citations**
- Multiple sources from same author – chronological order, separated by comma Example: (Burke, 1998, 1999, in press)
- Within same year: Example: (Burke, 1998a, 1998b, 1999, in press)
- Multiple sources – separated by semicolon, alphabetical order Example: (Burke, 1998; Perez, 1992; Wilhite, 2001)
- Personal communication (not included in references)
- Example: (T.K. Lutes, personal communication, September 19, 2001)

1. **Guilbert,J. (2008):**Educational Hand Book for Health personnel 6 th ed., printed in Switzerland by: Imprimaries popular , Geneda . Page (206) – (209-213-216).
2. **Jacobson, M., Pruitt Chapin, K., & Rugeley, C. (2009).** Toward Reconstructing Poverty Knowledge: Addressing Food Insecurity through Grassroots Research Design and Implementation. Journal of Poverty, 13(1), 1-19.
3. **Portney LG, Watkins MP. (2000).** *Foundations of Clinical Research: applications to practice.* 2nd Ed. Upper Saddle River, NJ: Prentice Hall Health.
4. **Hulley SB, Cummings SR. (1998).** *Designing Clinical Research: an epidemiologic approach.* Baltimore, MD: Williams and Wilkins.
5. **Cook TD, Campbell DT. (1979).** *Quasi-Experimentation: design & analysis issues for field settings.* Boston, MA: Houghton Mifflin Company.
6. **LoBiondo-Wood & Haber. (2006).** Nursing Research: Methods and Critical Appraisal for Evidence-Based Practice, 6th ed. USA: Mosby Inc.
7. • **Polit & Beck. (2008).** Nursing Research: Generating and Assessing Evidence for Nursing Practice, 8th ed. Philadelphia: Lippincott Williams & Wilkins.

CONTENT

More
Books!

OMNIScriptum

Printed by Books on Demand GmbH, Norderstedt / Germany